What do you see in the street?

Useful words

street
shop
house
school
church
factory

What can you see from the top of the hill?

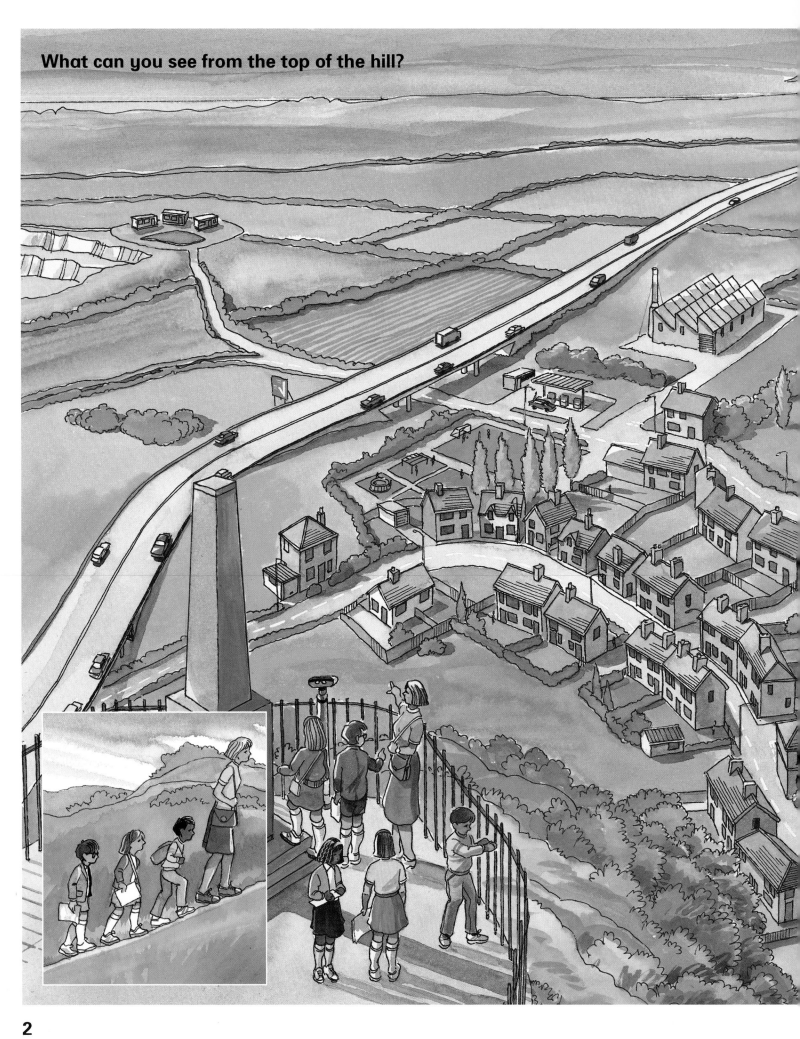

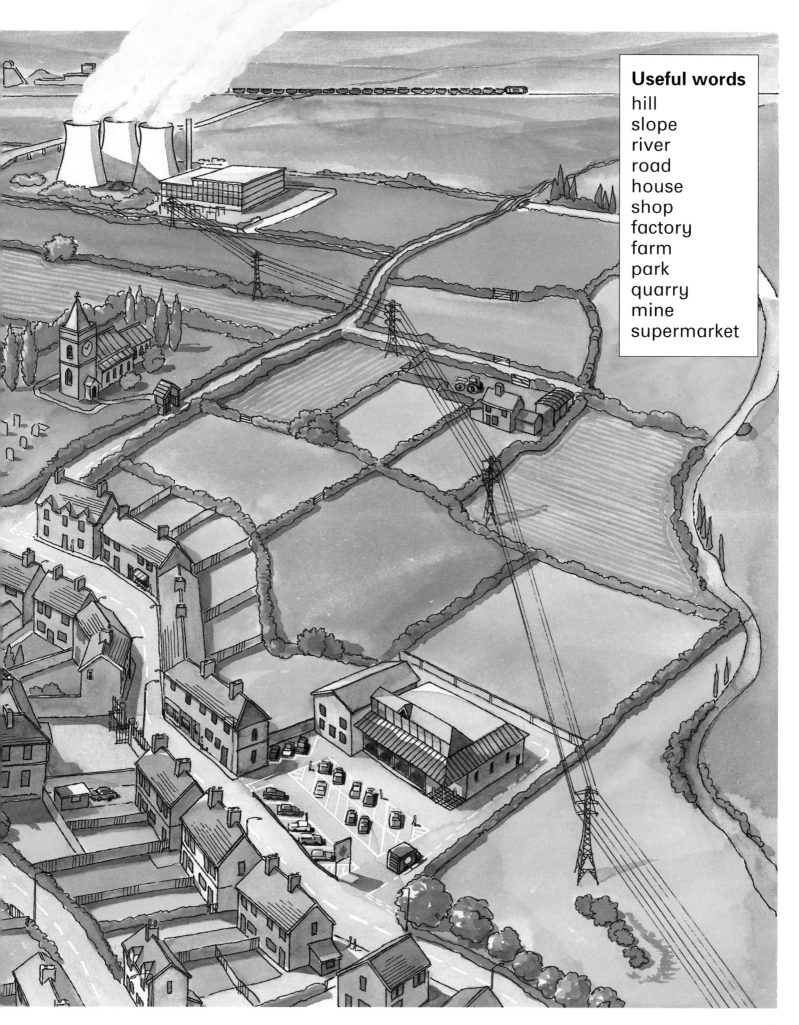

Useful words
hill
slope
river
road
house
shop
factory
farm
park
quarry
mine
supermarket

What can you see from the aeroplane?

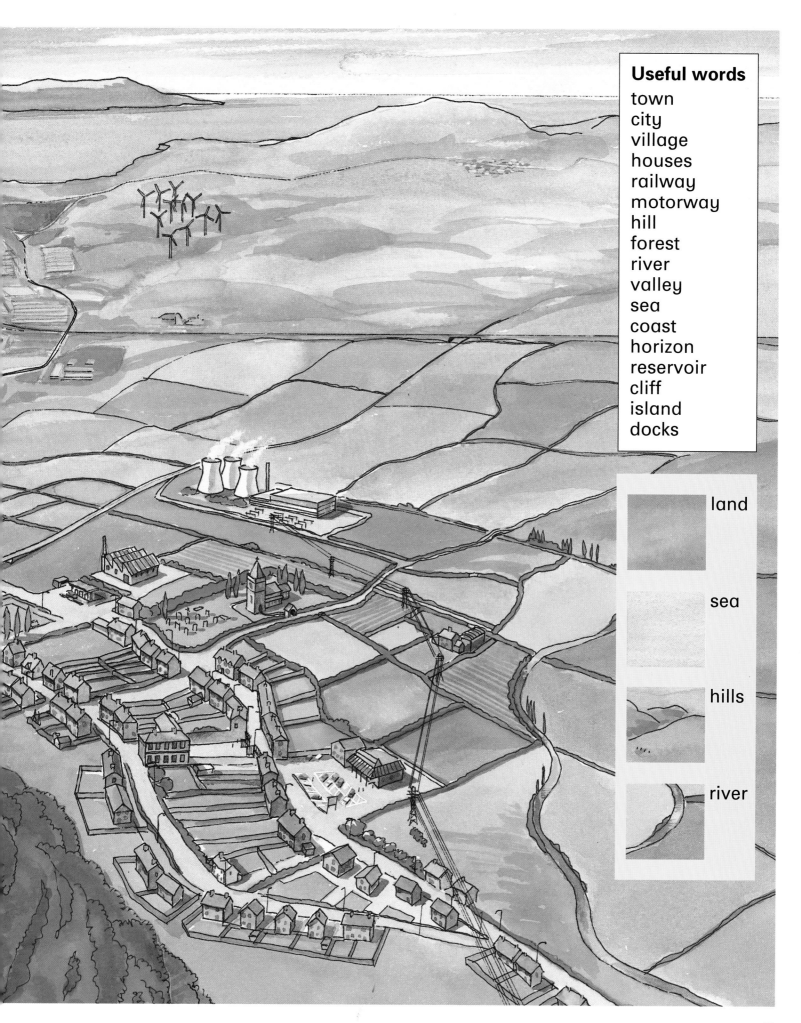

Useful words

town
city
village
houses
railway
motorway
hill
forest
river
valley
sea
coast
horizon
reservoir
cliff
island
docks

land

sea

hills

river

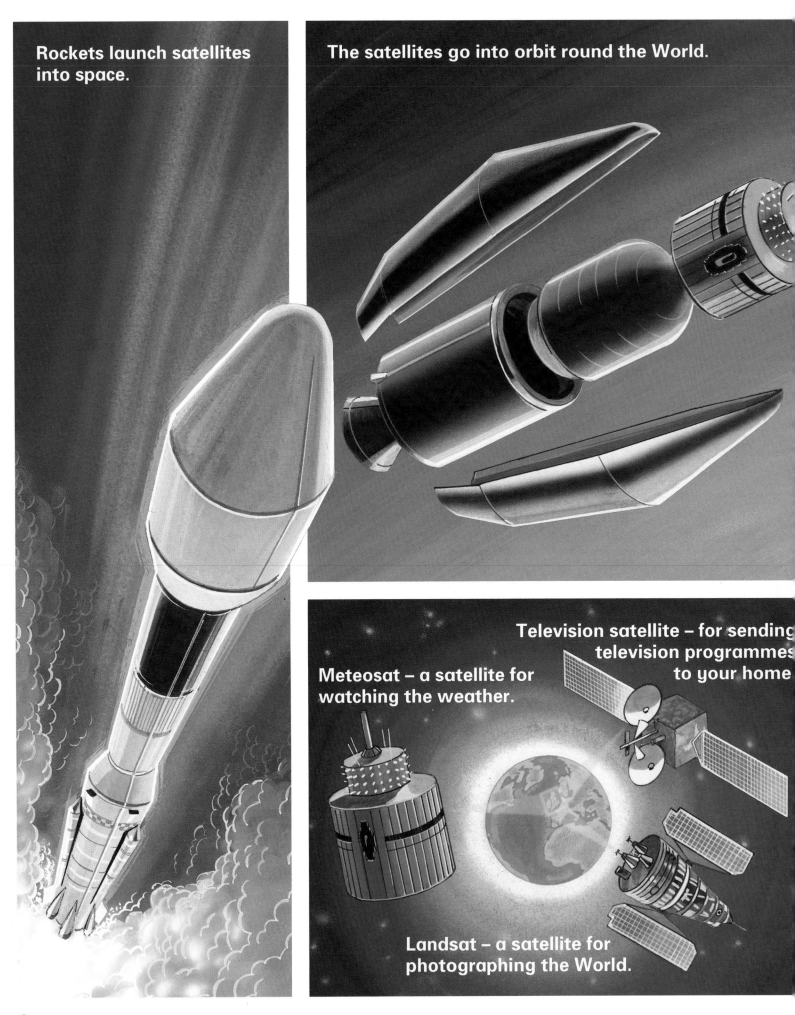

Rockets launch satellites into space.

The satellites go into orbit round the World.

Television satellite – for sending television programmes to your home

Meteosat – a satellite for watching the weather.

Landsat – a satellite for photographing the World.

What can you see from the satellite in space?

Look at a globe.
This is how a satellite
sees the World.

The space shuttle carries
people into space to
mend satellites.

land   sea

WHERE WE LIVE
The British Isles

This is a photo from a satellite. Can you see where you live?

The next page shows a map of the British Isles.

It is a drawing of the things you can see on the satellite photo.

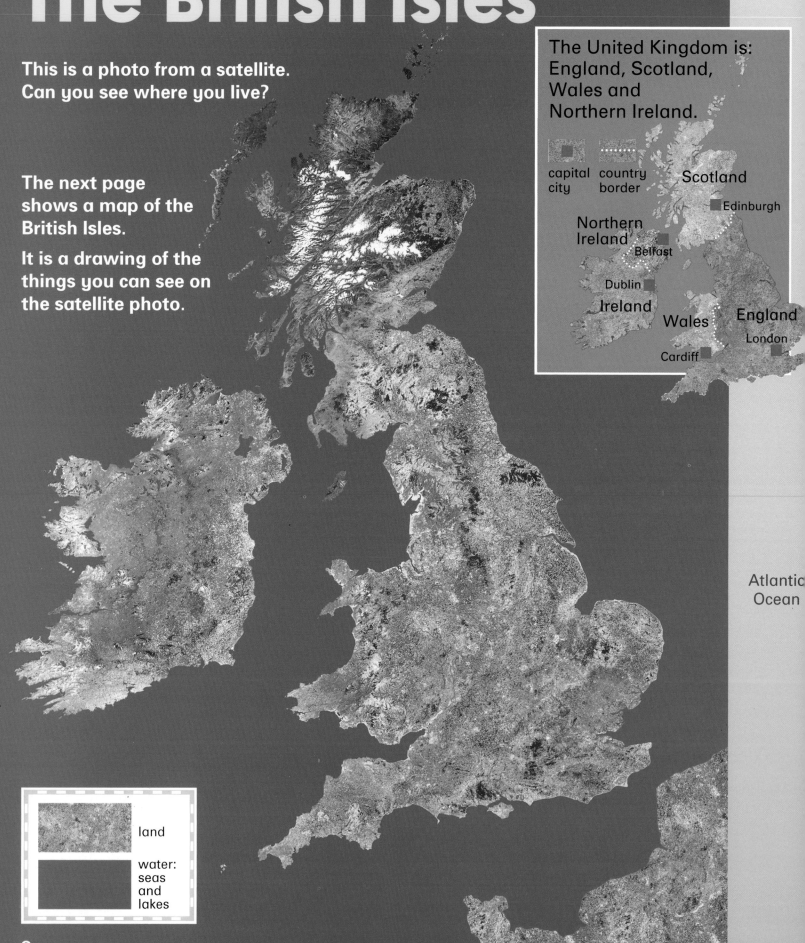

The United Kingdom is: England, Scotland, Wales and Northern Ireland.

capital city   country border

Scotland

Edinburgh

Northern Ireland

Belfast

Dublin

Ireland

Wales

England

London

Cardiff

Atlantic Ocean

land

water: seas and lakes

Which of these things on the map are near to where you live?

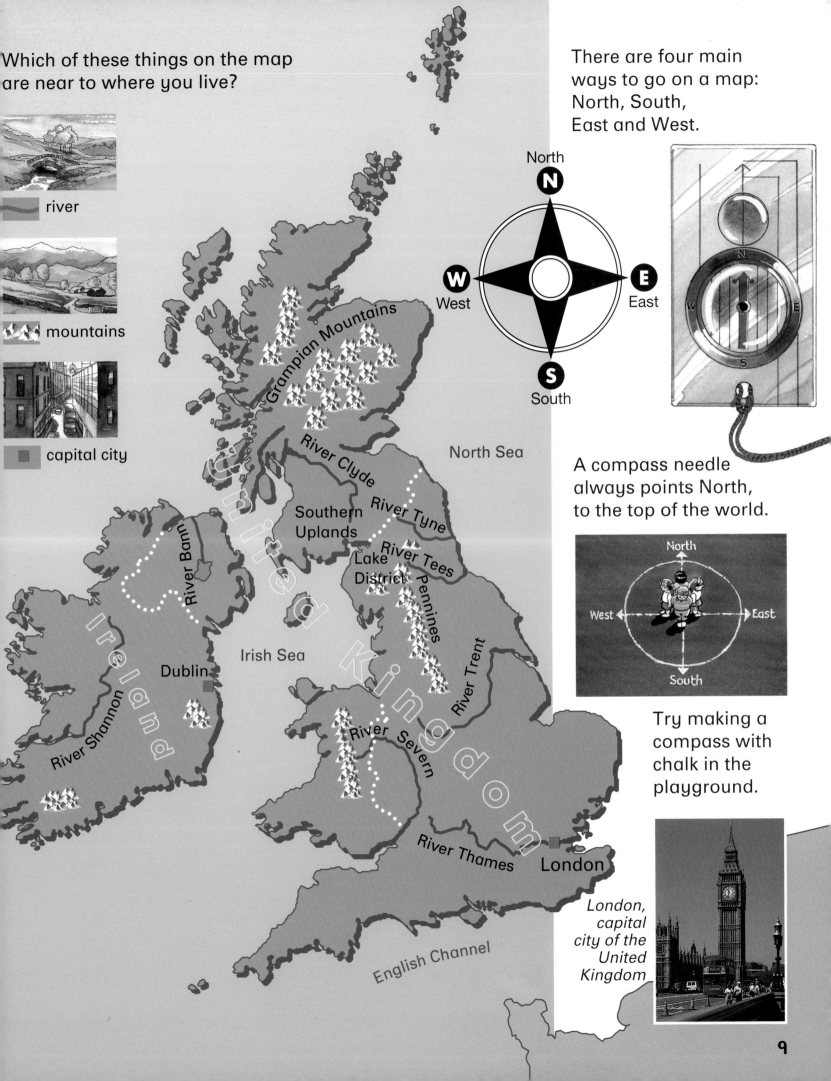

river

mountains

capital city

There are four main ways to go on a map: North, South, East and West.

North
N
W West   East **E**
S
South

A compass needle always points North, to the top of the world.

North
West   East
South

Try making a compass with chalk in the playground.

Grampian Mountains

River Clyde

North Sea

River Tyne

Southern Uplands

River Tees

Lake District

Pennines

River Bann

Ireland

River Shannon

Irish Sea

Dublin

River Trent

River Severn

River Thames   London

English Channel

London, capital city of the United Kingdom

Europe

N

The British Isles are part of the **continent** of Europe.

A continent is a big piece of land. There are six other continents besides Europe.

These foods come from Europe. Which ones have you tasted?

grapes, oranges, lettuce, apples, mushrooms, lemons, tomatoes, kiwi fruit, pears, cheese, celery, courgettes, cucumber and strawberries

North Sea

United Kingdom
London

Moscow

Russ

Berlin **Poland**

Germany

River Rhine

Europe

Paris

France

River Danube

Ukraine

Alps

Rome

Madrid

Italy

Spain

Mediterranean Sea

river

mountains

capital city

cool forest

country borders

Vineyards in Europe

The Alps

River Rhine

A street in Paris

A street in Berlin

These are some of the animals that live in Europe.

bat, stork, mole
puffin, hedgehog,
grey seal and deer

Africa

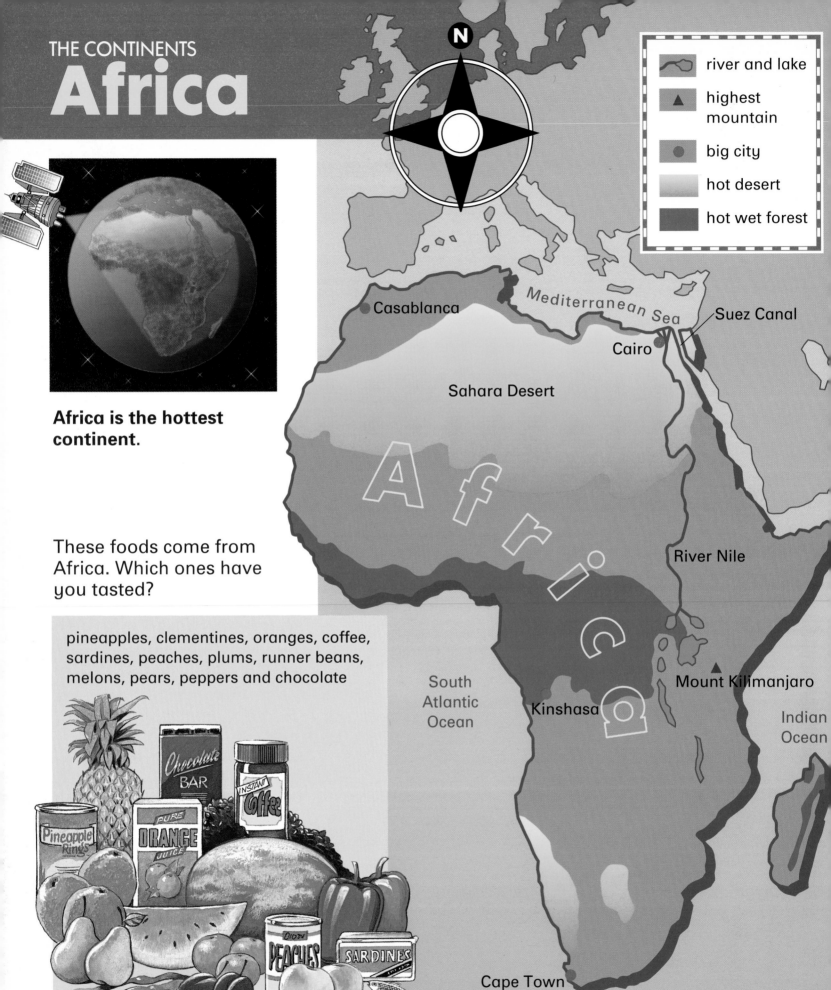

Africa is the hottest continent.

These foods come from Africa. Which ones have you tasted?

pineapples, clementines, oranges, coffee, sardines, peaches, plums, runner beans, melons, pears, peppers and chocolate

N

	river and lake
▲	highest mountain
●	big city
	hot desert
	hot wet forest

Casablanca

Mediterranean Sea

Suez Canal

Cairo

Sahara Desert

Africa

River Nile

South Atlantic Ocean

Kinshasa

Mount Kilimanjaro

Indian Ocean

Cape Town

River Nile

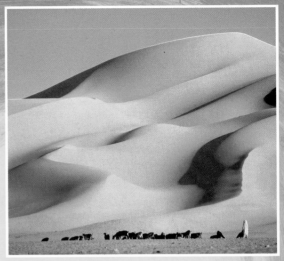
Sahara Desert

Mount Kilimanjaro

Suez Canal

A street in Cairo

Hot wet

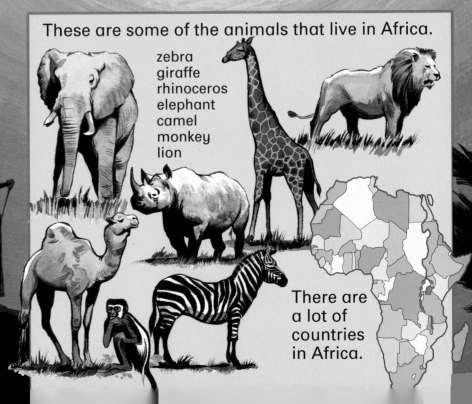

These are some of the animals that live in Africa.

zebra
giraffe
rhinoceros
elephant
camel
monkey
lion

There are a lot of countries in Africa.

Asia

Lake in Russia

Russia

Asia

Asia is the biggest continent.

It has the highest mountains.

These foods come from Asia. Which ones have you tasted?

Tehran
Baghdad

Himalayas

River Ganges

Mount Everest

China

Beijing

Seoul

India

Bombay

Calcutta

Indian Ocean

Jakarta

rice, mango, tea, ginger, dates and spices

RICE PUDDING

Ginger

DATES

River Ganges

Cold desert

Himalaya Mountains

Arctic Ocean

Tokyo
Japan

Pacific
Ocean

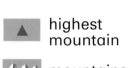
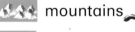
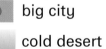

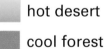

	river and lake
	highest mountain
	mountains
	big city
	cold desert
	hot desert
	cool forest
	hot wet forest

Hot wet forest

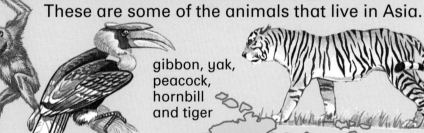
A street in Seoul

These are some of the animals that live in Asia.

gibbon, yak,
peacock,
hornbill
and tiger

*A street in
Tokyo*

There are
a lot of
countries
in Asia.

North and South America

America is two continents.

North America is the richest continent.

These foods come from North and South America. Which ones have you tasted?

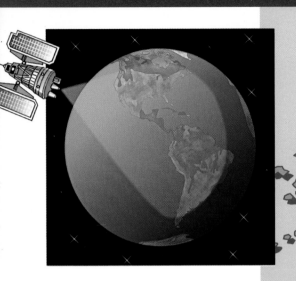

Rocky mountains

North America – corn on the cob, peanuts, popcorn, salmon, baked beans, rice, tuna, cornflakes (maize) and grapefruit

CORN FLAKES

SALMON

Rice

BAKED BEANS

Tuna

BEANS

Mild COFFEE

DRINKING Chocolate

STRONG COFFEE

CORNED Beef

South America – coffee, pears, corned beef, chocolate, bananas, paw paws, beans and limes

North America

Canada

Rocky Mountains

Chicago

United States

New York

Los Angeles

Mississippi River

North Atlantic Ocean

Mexico City

Caribbean Sea

Panama Canal

River Amazon

Pacific Ocean

Andes

South America

R

São Paulo

Bueno Aires

South Atlantic Ocean

	river and lake
	mountains
	big city
	hot desert
	cool forest
	hot wet forest

N

A street in New York

Mississippi River

Panama Canal

Andes Mountains

River Amazon

e Janeiro

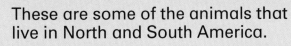

These are some of the animals that
live in North and South America.

NORTH – bald eagle,
raccoon, moose and
alligator

SOUTH –
macaw, toucan,
anteater and chinchilla

These
are the
countries
in North
and South
America.

Australasia

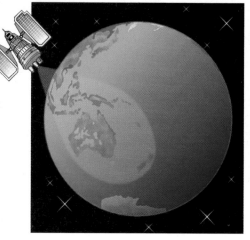

Australasia is the smallest continent.

It has the fewest people.

It is opposite the British Isles on the globe.

These foods come from Australasia. Which ones have you tasted?

butter, pears, peaches, apples, grapes and kiwi fruit

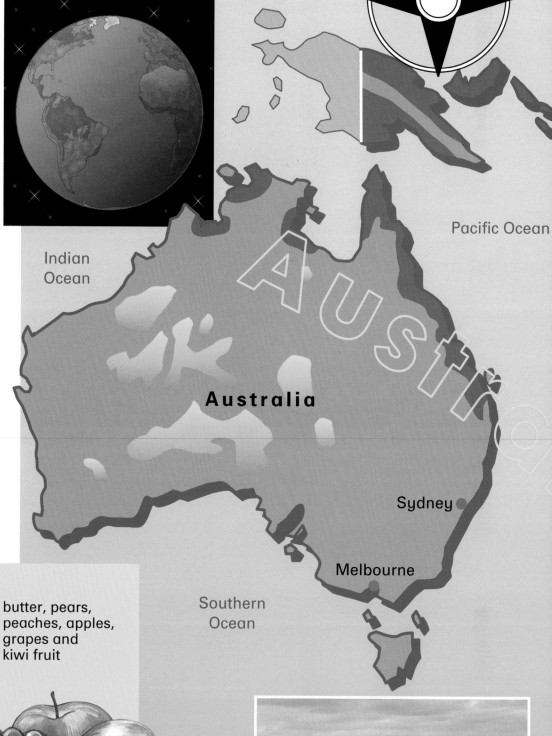

N

Pacific Ocean

Indian Ocean

Australia

AUST...

Sydney

Melbourne

Southern Ocean

Surfers on the Pacific coast

Hot wet forest

Travelling to a mine

Edge of the hot desert

Australian sheep farm

Panning for gold

A street in Sydney

New Zealand

These are some of the animals that live in Australasia.

albatross, koala bear, kangaroo, kookaburra, kiwi and shark

Australia is the biggest country in Australasia.

	hot wet forest
	hot desert
	big city

Antarctica and the South Pole

Antarctica is the coldest continent.

There are four months in winter when there is no daylight at all.

A few scientists live here from time to time.

Atlantic Ocean

sea

ice

To British Isles

To Africa

Indian Ocean

To S. America

Antarctica

N

N

N

N

South Pole

To Asia

To N. America

To Australasia

Southern Ocean

These are some of the animals that live at the South Pole.

skua, weddell seal, blue whale, sperm whale and emperor penguin

Which continents are near Antarctica?

Pacific Ocean

Coast of Antarctica

20

Near the North Pole

There is no land at the North Pole.

There is only the Arctic Ocean.

It is covered in a thick layer of ice.

No one lives here.

Pacific Ocean

	sea
	ice

North America

Arctic Ocean

Asia

To Australasia

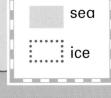

S

S   S

S

North Pole

To S. America

Greenland

To Africa

These are some of the animals that live at the North Pole.

arctic hare, arctic tern, ermine (stoat), arctic fox, polar bear and lemming

Atlantic Ocean

Which continents can you see around the North Pole?

Europe

21

The World

The World is round, like an orange.

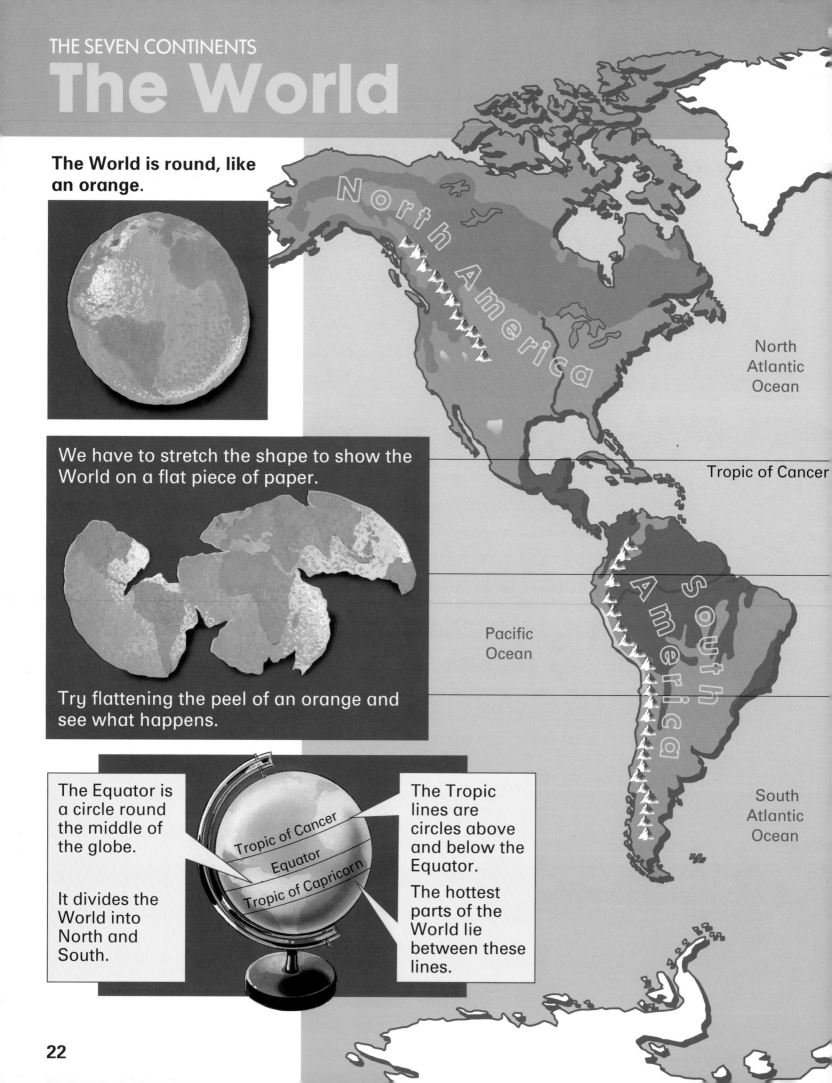

We have to stretch the shape to show the World on a flat piece of paper.

Try flattening the peel of an orange and see what happens.

The Equator is a circle round the middle of the globe.

It divides the World into North and South.

Tropic of Cancer

Equator

Tropic of Capricorn

The Tropic lines are circles above and below the Equator.

The hottest parts of the World lie between these lines.

North America

North Atlantic Ocean

Tropic of Cancer

South America

Pacific Ocean

South Atlantic Ocean

North Pole

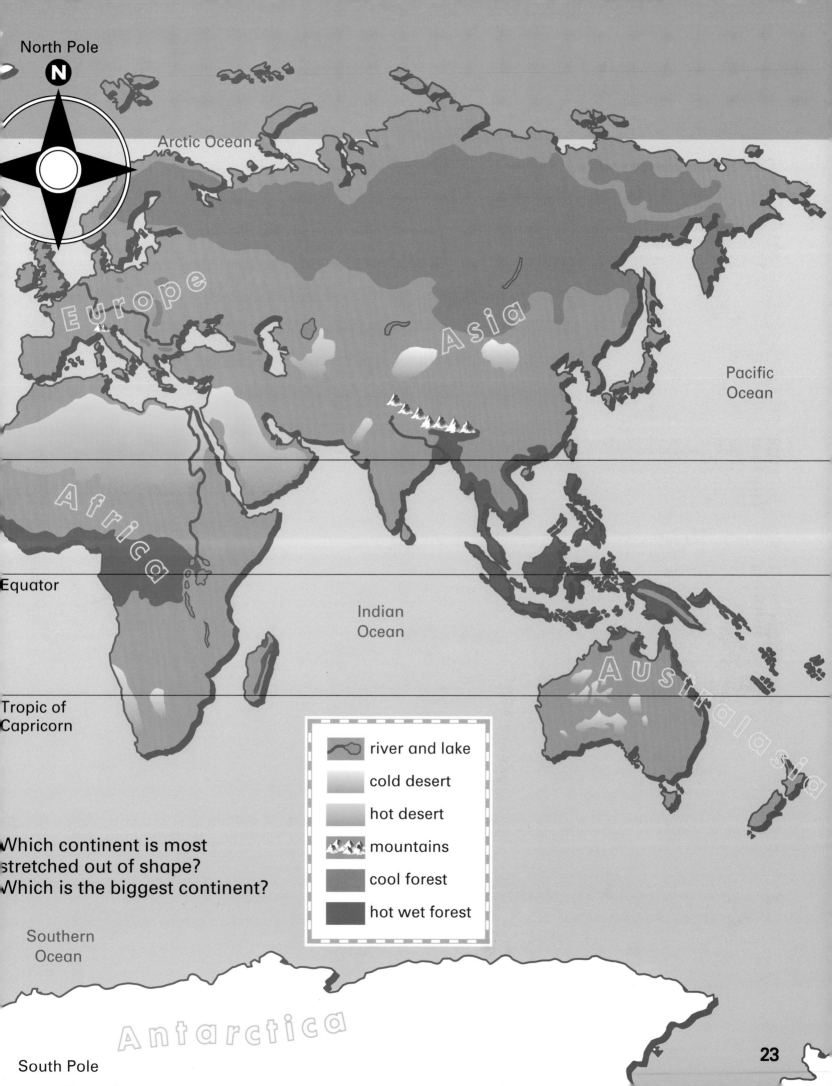

N

Arctic Ocean

Europe

Asia

Pacific
Ocean

Africa

Equator

Indian
Ocean

Australasia

Tropic of
Capricorn

Which continent is most
stretched out of shape?
Which is the biggest continent?

Southern
Ocean

river and lake

cold desert

hot desert

mountains

cool forest

hot wet forest

Antarctica

South Pole

23

Which continent would you most like to visit?

What do tourists go to see there?